INVESTIGATE! RELIGIONS

Original French text © 2019 Sophie de Mullenheim
Illustrations © 2019 Sophie Chaussade
English translation by Deborah Lock
This edition copyright © 2021 Lion Hudson IP Limited

All rights reserved. No part of this publication may be reproduced or transmitted in any form or by any means, electronic or mechanical, including photocopy, recording, or any information storage and retrieval system, without permission in writing from the publisher.

Published by
Lion Hudson Limited
Wilkinson House, Jordan Hill Business Park
Banbury Road, Oxford OX2 8DR, England
www.lionhudson.com
ISBN 978 0 74597 944 1

Originally published in French under the title Enquête sur les religions
by Sophie de Mullenheim (text) and Sophie Chaussade (illustrations)
Enquête sur les religions © First published in French by Mame, Paris, France - 2019
First English language edition 2021

Acknowledgments
Bible quotations taken from the Holy Bible, New International Version Anglicised.
Copyright © 1979, 1984, Biblica, formerly International Bible Society.
Used by permission of Hodder & Stoughton Ltd, an Hachette UK company.
All rights reserved. "NIV" is a registered trademark of Biblica. UK trademark number 1448790.

A catalogue record for this book is available from the British Library
Printed and bound in China, February 2021, LH54

Sophie de Mullenheim • Sophie Chaussade

INVESTIGATE! RELIGIONS

THE JEWISH, CHRISTIAN, AND MUSLIM FAITHS

LION CHILDREN'S

The authors of *Enquête sur les religions* wish to thank Mr Tareq Oubrou, Grand Imam of Bordeaux Mosque, theologian, thinker, and author for his careful rereading of the entire book. They also thank Stephanie, her family, and the rest of her community for their help and rereading of parts of the book devoted to Judaism. The publisher would like to thank Claire Clinton Director of Religious Education and RSHE, RE Matters.

CONTENTS

◆◆◆

1 What are the origins of the religions?......... 6
2 How are the religions different?......... 10
3 What is God named?..... 14
4 Why is Abraham the father of three faiths?..... 16
5 Is it true that Jesus was Jewish?.......... 18
6 What are the holy books?.. 20
7 What are the holy cities?. 24
8 Can believers do what they want?....... 28
9 What is a pilgrimage?... 30
10 What are the symbols of the faiths?........ 32
11 How do believers pray?... 34
12 Imam, Rabbi, Priest: who are they?...... 38
13 How do people become believers?......... 40
14 Is there a school to learn about God? 42

15 What are the important stages in the life of a believer?........ 44
16 Does God forgive?..... 48
17 Which day is special?... 50
18 What does a place of worship look like?.... 54
19 When do they celebrate festivals?......... 58
20 Does everyone give presents at Christmas?... 63
21 Are Lent and Ramadan the same thing?...... 65
22 Can believers eat what they like?......... 67
23 What happens after death?. 69
24 Does the devil exist?... 72
25 Which is the right religion?.......... 74

More useful words...... 76

INDEX 77

What are the origins of
THE RELIGIONS?

Through the ages, people have believed in one or more greater powers than themselves. For example, the ancient Egyptians, Greeks, and the Incas worshipped many gods with extraordinary powers.

THE START OF A ONE-GOD RELIGION

The Jewish religion began with God revealing himself to a man named Abraham. God told Abraham that he was the only God. The Jewish believe God gave land, laws, and prophets to the descendants of Abraham. Abraham lived around 1850 BC, but the first principles of Judaism were written down from 587 BC.

Useful words

Monotheism: a belief that there is only one God. Judaism, Christianity, and Islam are the three monotheistic religions.

Prophet: a person who speaks in the name of God.

A PROMISE

The Jewish prophets spoke about God's promise to save them. Christianity began with the coming of Jesus in the first century. Many Jews did not recognize him as the promised Messiah (Saviour). But others saw him as Christ, the one blessed by God, and decided to follow him and become his disciples. These first Christians believed Jesus to be God's Son.

AND WHY...

is Judaism so-called?
Among the descendants of Abraham was Jacob, who had twelve sons, including one named Judah. The land his descendants received was called Judah and the term Jew means "from the kingdom of Judah". Over time, this came to include all descendants of Abraham and their religion became known as Judaism.

A NEW RELIGION

Islam means "submitting to the will of God". This religion began with the Prophet Muhammad receiving revelations from God through the angel Gabriel. Muhammad began to preach in Mecca (now in Saudi Arabia), but his teachings about one God were not welcomed and so he was invited to the city of Medina in 622. His followers are called Muslims.

✓ TO READ ABOUT
THE HOLY BOOKS FOR EACH RELIGION,
GO TO...

6

✓ TO FIND OUT ABOUT
GROUPS WITHIN THE THREE RELIGIONS,
GO TO...

2

Identity cards

◆◆◆

The great figures of the monotheistic religions are sometimes known to each other.

ABRAHAM

Wife: Sarah
Descendants: Ishmael and Isaac... and all the believers.
Significant event: Abraham is the father of the three religions. He believes in following one God. God promises him many descendants and Abraham believes this although he is very old.
Other names: Muslims name him Ibrahim.

ISAAC

Father: Abraham
Mother: Sarah
Descendants: Esau and Jacob
Significant event: God asks Abraham to sacrifice Isaac as a test of his commitment to God. Abraham is about to do this when an angel stops him.

ISHMAEL

Father: Abraham
Mother: Hagar, the Egyptian servant of Sarah
Descendants: For Muslims, Ishmael is an ancestor to Muhammad.
Significant event: He is the eldest son to Abraham. Hagar and Ishmael are sent into the wilderness after Isaac's birth. God provides water for them and promises him many descendants.

JACOB

Father: Isaac
Mother: Rebekah
Twin brother: Esau
Significant event: Jacob dreams of a ladder with angels going up and down to heaven, and God promises the land to his many descendants. Another time, Jacob fights a stranger all night. At dawn, Jacob realizes he has been wrestling with God. He is given a new name, Israel.

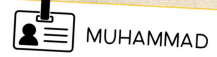
MUHAMMAD

Birthplace: Mecca
Date of death: 632 in Medina
Occupation: a merchant along trading routes
Significant event: Aged forty, Muhammad is visited by the angel Gabriel to receive the Word of God, the Qur'an, according to Muslims. Muhammad establishes the first Muslim state, Medina.

JESUS

Birthplace: Bethlehem
Mother: Mary
Adopted father: Joseph
Significant event: For Christians, Jesus is the Son of God who came to earth to save all people. He gave his life by being crucified and then rose from the dead to be alive again (resurrected) after three days.
Other name: Jews name him Yeshua and Muslims name him the Prophet Issa and he is their second most important prophet.

MARY

Husband: Joseph
Descendants: Jesus (God's Son), and four other sons
Significant event: Before she is married, Mary is visited by the angel Gabriel, who told her she was to be the mother of God's Son.
Other names: Muslims name her Maryam and she is mentioned more times in the Qur'an than in the Bible.

How are the religions DIFFERENT?

The religions of Jews, Christians, and Muslims have some similarities. Abraham is recognized as a father of the nations in all three religions. They are also monotheistic religions. This means they believe in only one God.

Useful words

Trinity: Christians believe in one God as three natures or persons: God the Father (Creator), God the Son (Jesus, God in human form), and God the Holy Spirit (how God works through the lives of Christians). This is called the mystery of the Trinity.

UNDERSTANDING GOD

Each of the monotheistic religions understands their one God differently. Believers from each religion relate to their one God differently. Jews believe that God not only created the universe, but every Jew can have an individual and personal relationship with God. They believe God continues to work in the world, affecting everything that people do. God speaks to them, protects them, leads them, and forgives them. The Jewish people have a covenant relationship with God, so in exchange for the good things God has done, the Jews keep God's laws and involve God in every aspect of their lives.

A WORD OF WISDOM

"Hear, O Israel, the Lord is our God, the Lord is one."
First line of the Jewish prayer called the Shema

BUT SO DIFFERENT

Christians also believe in a loving creator God with whom they can have a relationship, but God has gone further. Through Jesus, who Christians believe is God the Son, all people who follow him have been forgiven their wrongdoings and saved from death. This was done by Jesus coming to earth and offering his own life. They believe the Holy Spirit is God at work in the world and within people's lives as part of the relationship.

Muslims believe in a God as creator, but God does not become part of creation and is unknowable. They feel tiny before the unlimited power (omnipotence) and perfection of God and fully submit to doing God's will. The submission is not that of a slave before his master but rather that of a free man in front of his creator whom he trusts.

A WORD OF WISDOM

"For God so loved the world that he gave his one and only Son, that whoever believes in him shall not perish but have eternal life."
 The Gospel of John, chapter 3 verse 16

"Praise belongs to Allah, the Lord of the worlds, the Merciful, the Compassionate, the Master of the Day of Judgment."
 Surah al-fatiha opening chapter, the Qur'an

✓ TO FIND OUT MORE ABOUT THE FATHER OF THE THREE FAITHS, ABRAHAM, GO TO...

4

✓ TO DISCOVER THE CITY THAT IS HOLY TO THE THREE RELIGIONS, GO TO...

7

Who's Who?

In every religion, there are different movements or groups that have distinctive features and practices. Here are some of them.

JEWS

Orthodox Jews are those who observe the laws and rules of the religion in the strictest way.

Reform Jews hold central beliefs but allow personal choice in observing the law.

Conservative Jews accept the Law but believe this should adapt to current culture.

CHRISTIANS

The Roman Catholic Church is the largest of the Christian churches. The Greek word katholikos means "universal". Catholics are led by the authority of the pope.

The Orthodox Church developed from the separation in 1054 between the eastern and western Christians, who did not agree on certain points of the faith and the organization of the church. They are found mainly in eastern Europe and western Asia.

The Protestant churches have been founded since the time of Reformation (14th–15th centuries) when people "protested" against the Catholic Church in Europe. They focus on the importance of the Bible and preaching God's Word. Many Protestants are known as evangelical Christians.

MUSLIMS

In 632, after Muhammad's death, Muslims did not agree about who should succeed the Prophet.

Sunni Muslims see the succession as a political decision to be debated and elected. Abu Bakr, a close companion of the Prophet, became the First Caliph (successor).

Shi'a Muslims believe Muhammad appointed his son-in-law and cousin, Ali, as successor to be their spiritual guide. Their leaders are imams, who are appointed from the Prophet's descendants and are believed to be faultless.

3 What is GOD NAMED?

You may call your father "Daddy", but if he meets a friend in the street, then he will be called by his first name. Perhaps at work, some may call him "Sir". People relate to him in different ways. With religions, people's relationship to God is not the same. Their way of addressing their God varies from one religion to another.

HASHEM

Jews believe that no one can see God, approach him, or even pronounce his name. In the Jewish tradition, God makes himself known under a name that Jews never say. When they talk about God, they use HaShem, which means "the name".

AN INFINITE NUMBER OF NAMES

Among Muslims, God is Allah, which is the Arabic translation of the word. But this name is not enough because it does not state who God is. So, Muslims have an infinite number of names given to God, such as the Almighty, the All-Merciful, the Creator, the Righteous, the One. Each name says something about the many qualities of God for Muslims, and how they should respond.

TRINITY GOD

Christians love their God, who is one God in three persons. For them, God is Father, Son, and Holy Spirit. God the Son is also known as Christ, the Lord, who is Jesus. The name used depends on the situation and what they want to express. Sometimes a Christian may want to call God a familiar "Dad" or talk to him saying a worshipful "my God" or "Lord".

MYSTERIOUS...

When the prophet Moses asked God what he was called, God replied, "I AM WHO I AM". Jews translated this answer with a word that does not have vowels: YHWH. They write the name in English as G-D. When Jews read texts of their holy book, the Torah, aloud they do not pronounce that name if it is written in the text. Instead, they replace it with "Adonai", a Hebrew word for "my Lord" and continue the reading.

✓ TO FIND OUT HOW PEOPLE PRAY TO GOD,
GO TO...
11

✓ TO DISCOVER MORE ABOUT JESUS,
GO TO...
5

Why is Abraham the FATHER OF THREE FAITHS?

For the believers of the Jewish, Christian, and Muslim religions, Abraham is an important figure. God promised him descendants that were as many as the stars in the sky and grains of sand in the desert.

ONE PATRIARCH

Jews and Christians consider Abraham as the father of their faiths, for God made a covenant or promise with him that forms the special relationship. At first named Abram, which in Hebrew means "exalted father", God gave him a new name, Abraham, when the covenant was made, promising him to be the "father of many" nations. The Jewish people are descendants of his son, Isaac. Muslims know Abraham as Ibrahim, an important prophet. The Arab people are descendants of his first son, Ishmael.

TWO FAMILIES

Abraham had a wife named Sarah. Although God promised Abraham many descendants, they continued to have no children and were getting old. Knowing this, Abraham had a son with Sarah's maid, Hagar. This son was named Ishmael. Later, Sarah did become pregnant in her old age and she gave another son to Abraham, named Isaac. For Jews and Christians, the story continues that one day, God asks Abraham to sacrifice his son, Isaac, as a test of trust and faithfulness. Abraham obeys and puts his son on the altar and prepares to kill him when an angel stops him, and God provides a ram caught in the thicket to be sacrificed instead. For Christians, this story has added significance, as it links to the self-sacrifice of God's Son, Jesus, on the cross. For Muslims, in the Qur'an, Ibrahim has a dream in which he sees himself preparing to sacrifice his son. After consulting his son, the sacrifice is prepared, and God appears in a vision to prevent it. The Qur'an does not name the son, the sacrifice is less terrifying, and this act of sacrifice was not directly given by God.

Useful words

Covenant: This is an agreement. Jews and Christians believe God promised land and blessings to Abraham's descendants and to be their God; in return they were to keep obeying God.

MYSTERIOUS...

The story of the sacrifice of Abraham's son may shock you. At the time of Abraham, other religions held human sacrifices and so religious experts explain this story as a way to teach that God for each of these three religions does not want human sacrifices. For Christians, this story has added significance, as God providing a ram to sacrifice instead of Isaac links to the self-sacrifice of God's Son, Jesus, on the cross.

✓ TO FIND OUT ABOUT IMPORTANT FIGURES, GO TO...

1

✓ TO DISCOVER WHERE TO HEAR ABRAHAM'S STORY, GO TO...

14

Is it true that
JESUS WAS JEWISH?

Mary, the mother of Jesus, was Jewish, so Jesus was born a Jew. Mary was married to Joseph, who was descended from the Israelite King David. Jesus was born in Bethlehem, a Jewish town that was the hometown of David. When still a new-born baby, Jesus was taken to the Temple in the city of Jerusalem to be presented, according to Jewish tradition. Jesus grew up as a Jew in the Jewish town of Nazareth. He learned how to pray with psalms (sacred songs), and was taught the ancient holy texts, the commandments of God, and the history of Israel and the Hebrew people. He went to the synagogue, the Jewish place of worship. At the age of twelve, he joined his parents on a pilgrimage to Jerusalem. He celebrated the Jewish holidays, including the Passover festival. He knew passages from the Torah, the Jewish holy book, by heart. Jesus was a committed Jew.

Useful words

Gentile: At the time of Jesus, all the people who were not Jewish were known as "Gentiles". For the first time, Jesus' message about God was shared with them.

JEWISH BELIEVER

Jesus was Jewish, and for Christians, this is very important. They believe that Jesus came to complete the great story of the covenant and love between God and the people of Israel. Jesus did not change the Jewish laws or traditions but respected them, and even accused the religious leaders of his time of being hypocrites and not being true to their faith. Jesus also went further, for his message was not just for the Jewish people but for all people. This was confusing for the Jews of his time who believed they were the specially chosen people of God.

PROPHECIES

Christians believe that the life of Jesus was announced centuries before he was born by the Jewish prophets. He was born in the town of the great King David as foretold, he suffered and died as they had proclaimed, and he is resurrected (raised to life) according to their holy writings. Through what Jesus did and said, his followers (the disciples) understood him to be the one that the Jewish prophets announced was coming: the Messiah, God's Son. These disciples became the first Christians.

AND WHAT...

was Jesus' message?
Jesus taught about the kingdom of God. He spoke about what God was like and told people how to change their lives around to live as friends of God.

✓ TO FIND OUT HOW THE BIRTH OF JESUS IS CELEBRATED, GO TO...

20

✓ TO READ ABOUT BELIEFS ON LIFE AFTER DEATH, GO TO...

23

What are the HOLY BOOKS?

Jews, Christians, and Muslims have their own holy book – books that contain God's message to people – guiding how to live their daily life as believers. There are some common stories within the texts that are almost the same but have been interpreted in different ways by each religion.

IN THE BEGINNING

For Jews, not all the texts in the Hebrew Bible, or Tanakh, hold the same importance. The most important texts are the first five books that make up the Torah, which means "teaching". These contain the early history of the Jewish religion and God's laws on how to live a good and faithful life. Jews believe the words were revealed to the prophet Moses. The Torah is handwritten on a long parchment wrapped around two rollers. The whole scroll is read over the course of a year at the synagogue. The text is written in Hebrew with no punctuation or vowels. The scrolls are handwritten and a copy can take up to two years to make. To follow the text, the reader uses a special stick called a "yad" to point to the words and prevent the text from being damaged.

THE STORY CONTINUES

The Torah of the Hebrew Bible also forms the first five books of the Old Testament in the Christian Bible. The other two books of the Hebrew Bible – Nevi'im (the Prophets) and Ketuvim (the Writings) – make up the rest of the Old Testament, but some of the books are placed in a different order. This continues the story of God with the Jewish people, including their exile and return to Jerusalem. The New Testament, originally written in Greek, begins with the coming of Jesus when God starts a new covenant relationship with all people. The first four books are known as the Gospels and recount the life of Jesus. Then there is the story of the early Christians, followed by letters and writings of these first Christians, providing guidance to the earliest church communities. The Bible ends with a book of Revelation of the end of times. There are sixty-six books in the Bible, but the Catholic Bible includes an additional seven books in the Old Testament. Passages are read aloud during services. They are made easier to read by being divided into chapters and verses.

PROFILE

In the late fourteenth century, Saint Jerome translated the Bible into Latin, and his version, known as the Vulgate, was considered the most accurate. This was the text used for the first printed Bible created by Johannes Gutenberg in 1454–1455.

LISTENING TO THE ANGEL

Among the sacred books for Muslims is the Tawrat, which is the Jewish Torah given to the prophet Musa (Moses), and the Zabur, which are the psalms given to the prophet Dawud (David), and found in the Jewish Tanakh and the Christian Bible. For Muslims, the most sacred book is the Qur'an, which they believe contains God's final revelation to people. The archangel Gabriel appeared to the Prophet Muhammad and dictated the words. The visits continued for twenty-two years before the text of the Qur'an was complete. The Qur'an is written in Arabic and so reads from right to left. It is made up of 114 surahs, or chapters. The first surah is the one that every Muslim says in their five daily prayers. The sacred book is respected, and the writing learned by heart.

MYSTERIOUS...

Muslims believe the Qur'an was directly recited by God to Muhammad through the archangel Gabriel, so it is the language of God. The Jewish Torah is believed to be dictated by God to Moses, so it is also God's Word. Christians believe God inspired the various authors of the books of the Bible, so when it is read during services, the reader ends with saying, "This is the Word of the Lord". This is because the Bible "speaks" the Word of God.

✓ TO FIND OUT WHERE THESE WRITINGS ARE STUDIED, GO TO...

14

✓ TO DISCOVER WHERE THESE TEXTS ARE READ, GO TO...

18

But also...

In every religion, there are other books that are used to guide the lives of believers. These are some examples.

THE JEWISH TALMUD

The Jewish law is long and complicated. The first Jewish rabbis, or teachers, discussed how best to apply it. The Talmud is a text written by them that helps Jewish people understand the law and put it into practice.

THE CATECHISM OF THE CATHOLIC CHURCH

The Catechism is a book in which Catholic Christians can find all the instructions needed to live their faith. There are explanations of the church symbols, how to live as a Christian, apply God's commandments, and pray.

THE SUNNAH

Those who knew the Prophet Muhammad wrote about his life and his sayings to help believers better understand the Qur'an. These writings are called hadiths. These hadiths form the Sunnah, which contains all the rules of Islam and acts as the law for believers. The Sunnah also helps to explain many of the teachings of the Qur'an. For example, the five set prayer times during the day is a practice set in the Sunnah. The Sunnah covers the same subjects as the Qur'an, such as beliefs, religious and ethical practices, and accounts of prophets.

What are the
HOLY CITIES?

The three main monotheistic religions emerged first in the Middle East. This was the area where Abraham, Jesus, and Muhammad lived. So, it is in the Middle East where the most holy cities are located, including Jerusalem, which is important to each religion.

THE HOLY CITY OF JERUSALEM

The city of Jerusalem attracts Jewish, Christian, and Muslim believers. They come to gather at places that are symbolic to their religions. For Jews, Jerusalem is the place where Solomon, King of Israel, built the first Temple as a place of worship. Christians come to pray at the tomb of Jesus and at the different places he went to before he was crucified on the cross and then resurrected (raised to life). For Muslims, the Al-Aqsa Mosque in Jerusalem is the third holiest site, and the shrine called The Dome of the Rock marks the place where Muhammad ascended to heaven after the night journey from Mecca to Jerusalem.

Useful words

Pilgrimage: A journey, often made on foot, to a holy place as an act of prayer or devotion to God.

PILGRIMAGE CITIES

For Muslims, there are two more important sites than Jerusalem. Muhammad was born in Mecca in Saudi Arabia and in the centre of the city is the Ka'ba, a sacred shrine covered in black cloth. All over the world, Muslims turn towards Mecca to pray five times a day. Medina in Saudi Arabia is where Muhammad founded the first Muslim city. All Muslims aim to take a pilgrimage, or hajj, to both these cities at least once in their lives. For Jews and Christians, there are many holy places that are linked to people from the Bible. For example, in Hebron, south of Jerusalem, Jews visit the tombs of the patriarchs Abraham, Isaac, and Jacob. At Mount Sinai, the prophet Moses received the tablets of the law, known as the Ten Commandments. In Nazareth, Christians visit the church built over the home of Mary, and in Bethlehem, the Church of the Nativity marks the place where Jesus was born.

AND WHY...

do Catholic Christians go to Rome?
In the centre of the city of Rome in Italy is the State of the Vatican City. This is the smallest country in the world, and it is where the pope lives. In the Vatican is St Peter's Basilica, which was built over the tomb of Jesus' disciple St Peter, who founded the church after the death and resurrection of Jesus.

✓ TO FIND OUT ABOUT PILGRIMAGE, GO TO...
9

✓ TO DISCOVER PLACES OF WORSHIP, GO TO...
18

Map of Jerusalem

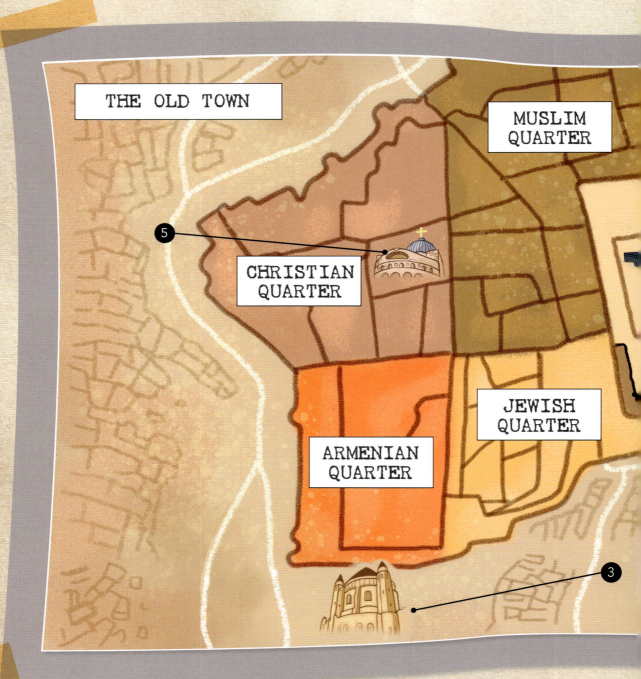

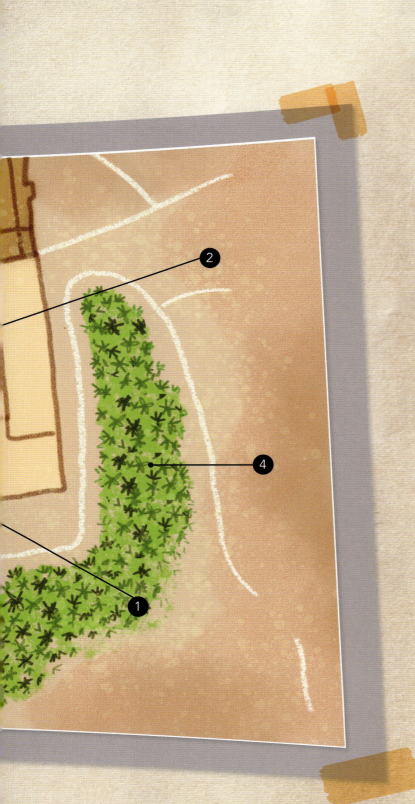

1. Only one wall remains from the ancient Temple built by Solomon and then rebuilt by Herod. This is called the Wailing Wall. Jews gather there and slip small pieces of paper with prayers written on between the stones.

2. The Dome of the Rock marks the place where Muhammad ascended to heaven in the company of the archangel Gabriel after his night journey from Mecca to Jerusalem.

3. In the Upper Room, Jesus shared his last meal with his disciples.

4. The Garden of Gethsemane is where Jesus spent his last night, praying before he was arrested.

5. The Church of the Holy Sepulchre marks the place where Jesus was buried after being crucified nearby at Mount Golgotha.

Can BELIVERS DO what they want?

For community life to work smoothly, a framework is needed. In a country, there are laws, rights, and responsibilities. In a family or at school, rules are set and followed. In every religion, there are commandments for living in harmony with God.

THE TEN COMMANDMENTS

Jews, Christians, and Muslims consider that the Ten Commandments given to Moses by God are important. "To love the Lord your God with all your might, you will not kill, you will not steal…" The Ten Commandments provide a firm foundation for leading a good life as a believer. But each religion has added to or adapted these commandments.

MANY LAWS

The Jews believe that God gave 613 commandments, which they call the mitzvot. These are found in the Torah and provide the rules on what the Jews can and cannot do. They give instructions on how to behave, their prayers, their food, and the way to dress. Among the most important laws is respecting Shabbat, or the Sabbath, the Jewish day of rest.

ESSENTIAL RULES

There are five essential requirements for Muslims, known as the Five Pillars of Islam. The first and most important is proclaiming their faith in one God and in the prophecy of Muhammad. The other aspects required are prayer, almsgiving, fasting, and the pilgrimage to Mecca. Muslims are expected to make these five points the foundation for their lives. There are other rules, including not drinking alcohol or eating pork.

MYSTERIOUS...

The 613 Jewish commandments are split into two groups: 248 positive commandments and 365 negative commandments. The positive "do" laws encourage ways to behave, and the negative "do not" laws prohibit others. These are not found in the Talmud, the book of Jewish law and explanations, but are included in different passages throughout the Torah. Rabbis, wise Jewish teachers, have gathered them in a list.

✓ TO FIND OUT HOW PEOPLE BECOME BELIEVERS, GO TO...

13

✓ TO DISCOVER RELIGIOUS LAWS ABOUT FOOD, GO TO...

22

FOLLOWERS

For Christians, they are free to live their faith according to their conscience. However, this conscience is based on trying to follow Jesus' teachings and apply them to their lives, particularly Jesus' simplified commandment: "Love one another as I have loved you." For example, Jesus showed great love for the poor, the sick, and the outcasts, so Christians follow this example through doing acts of kindness and supporting organizations that work to relieve suffering. Gathering to worship God, sharing bread and wine to remember Jesus, and praying as Jesus taught are part of a Christian's life.

What is a PILGRIMAGE?

Some trips are not like others. The destination is not a place for a holiday or to a famous cultural or natural site, but instead to a holy place. These trips are called pilgrimages. Believers go to an important place connected with their religion as part of an act of devotion to God.

CLOSER TO GOD

In many cases, the pilgrimage involves walking and the believer uses this slower pace to reflect on their life with God. The time is used to pray and share experiences of God with others. The effort is a way to get closer to God.

Three of the Jewish holidays were originally pilgrimage festivals – Passover, Shavuot, and Sukkot – and people used to walk from towns in the countryside to the Temple in Jerusalem to celebrate. Many Christians, especially Catholic Christians, go on pilgrimages to shrines to give thanks to God or ask for help or go to the Holy Land in the Middle East to visit sites mentioned in the Bible. Muslims are required to take a pilgrimage to Mecca involving a series of rituals as the final Pillar of Islam.

PILGRIMAGE SITES

In every religion and all around the world, there are places or holy cities that attract a very large number of pilgrims. These places have become holy because important events have happened there, or the places are linked with holy people.

MYSTERIOUS...

The Santiago de Compostela is a long pilgrimage walk starting in France and ending in northern Spain that some Christians make. It is so long that often pilgrims walk a bit every year and complete it over several years.

AND WHY...

do Muslims go to Mecca?
The pilgrimage, or hajj, to Mecca is one of the Five Pillars of Islam, which are essential requirements for believers. Each Muslim, if they are in good health and have the money, must do this great pilgrimage at least once in their lives. Hajj takes place every year and lasts several days. Millions of Muslims from around the world gather and circle around the Ka'ba, the black cubed building in the centre of the mosque. The Ka'ba is the sanctuary of God, thought to have been founded by Adam, the father of humankind, and rebuilt in honour of God by Ibrahim and his son Ishmael according to the Qur'an.

✓ TO FIND OUT ABOUT OTHER DUTIES OF BELIEVERS, GO TO...
8

✓ TO DISCOVER ABOUT RELIGIOUS FESTIVALS, GO TO...
19

What are the SYMBOLS OF THE FAITHS?

Each country has a flag symbolizing its national identity. In the past, knights had coats of arms to show who they were. In the same way, each religion has a symbol or symbols that marks them out. The sign also means something deeply significant.

STAR, PERFECT BALANCE

The Jewish religion is very often associated with the sign of the Star of David. This star with six branches is also known as Solomon's Seal. This star represents the balance that exists between heaven and earth, between what comes from God and what comes from humankind. The Star of David is not the only symbol of Jewish believers. The oldest Jewish religious sign is the menorah, the seven-branched candlestick that was lit in the Temple, symbolizing the nation of Israel as "God's light". Menorahs are found in each Jewish home.

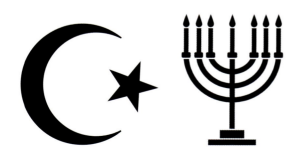

SAVIOUR'S CROSS

The main symbol of Christianity is the cross on which Jesus died. The cross is not a sign of torture but a symbol of deliverance, for in dying on the cross and then being resurrected (raised to life), Jesus saved people from the burden of their sin and death. Some Christians make the sign of the cross with their hand across their bodies, reaffirming that they believe in one God in three persons. Another symbol is a fish. The first letters in Greek for Jesus Christ, Son of God, Saviour, make ICHTHYS, which is the Greek word for fish. Jesus called his first disciples to follow him and become "fishers of people". Early Christians used this symbol to identify themselves.

UNDER THE SIGN OF THE MOON

The star and the crescent have been associated with the Muslim religion for a very long time, but this is not linked to Muhammad. This and other symbols are mostly cultural signs chosen by caliphates (elected leaders). To work out the dates of Muslim holidays, the lunar (moon's) calendar is used, so the crescent reflects the natural pace of life. The five-sided star represents the Five Pillars of Islam.

These religious signs are often used in jewellery or engraved on monuments so that believers wherever they are can feel that they belong to the same family of faith.

DID YOU KNOW?
The Red Cross is an international organization helping people around the world who are suffering. The founder was a Christian from Switzerland who chose a red cross on a white background, opposite to the Swiss flag. Since then, as the organization has developed, in Muslim countries the Red Crescent is used.

✓ TO FIND OUT THE NAMES GIVEN TO GOD, GO TO...
3

✓ TO DISCOVER ABOUT KEY STAGES OF LIFE FOR BELIEVERS, GO TO...
15

11 How do believers PRAY?

Whether Jewish, Christian, or Muslim, prayer is central to a believer's life. Prayer is when a believer speaks to God, and it is part of daily life. The religions vary about the guidance or even rules about how and when to pray.

Useful words

Amen: This little word, meaning "So be it", is used at the end of prayers. It asserts that everything that has just been said is true for the believer. This word is 'Ameen' in Arabic.

A BELIEVER'S DUTY

For Muslims, prayer is one of the Five Pillars of Islam, which are the five things Muslims must do in their lives. Prayer takes place five times a day: in the morning, around noon, in the afternoon, at sunset, and in the evening. Schedules are set according to a timetable that varies with the sun and the moon. Before praying, Muslims make their ablutions, which is a particular way of washing their forearms and their faces, wiping their hair with moistened hands, and washing their feet up to the ankles. If there is no water, they "wash" using a clean pebble. Then, turning towards Mecca, Muslims enter into prayer, which is like a place of confession (saying sorry) and intimacy with God. They use symbolic gestures and positions in a precise order with set words known as the rak'a. They begin standing, saying passages from the Qur'an, and end sitting in peace, having gone through bowing and prostrations. There are opportunities for Muslims to make their own silent personal prayers too.

FREE-FLOWING CONVERSATION

Many Christians pray whenever they want and for all sorts of reasons. Those in special religious communities have specific moments in the day devoted to prayer. Different groups of Christians may have a certain way of praying and an order in which to say prayers. Jesus taught his disciples how to pray beginning with the words "Our Father" and these words are used by all Christians. Christian prayers are free-flowing conversations, as if spending precious time with a close and respected family member. They pray from the heart to give thanks and praise to God, ask for forgiveness in Jesus' name and help in their own and others' lives around the world.

RESPECTFUL PRAYER

Jewish tradition is to pray three times a day: morning, afternoon, and evening. Male Jews may also follow a dress code, wearing a head covering known as a kippa and a prayer shawl called a tallit. For morning services, Orthodox Jews also wear a tefillin, which are two small black boxes. One is hung on the forehead close to the mind, and the other is hung on the left arm if they are right-handed or on the right arm if they are left-handed, close to the heart. These boxes contain passages from the Torah and the most important prayer text called the Shema written on parchments.

MYSTERIOUS

Muslims and Catholic Christians use a string of beads to help them pray. For Catholics, the beads, or rosary, represent three different prayers, helping them to keep count of the number of times they say the prayer as they meditate. For Muslims, a string of ninety-nine prayer beads, the subha, is a reminder of the divine names of Allah. They are separated every thirty-three beads with a different bead, with the first group repeating "Glory to Allah", the second group "Praise be to Allah", and the third group "Allah is Great". The beads can be used to count phrases in personal prayer, too.

✓ TO FIND OUT WHICH DAY OF THE WEEK IS THE MOST IMPORTANT.
GO TO...
17

✓ TO DISCOVER ABOUT PLACES OF WORSHIP, GO TO...
18

Prayers of the religions

Each of the religions has an important prayer that every believer says and often even learns to recite.

SHEMA ISRAEL (TRANSLATED FROM HEBREW)

Hear O Israel, the Lord is our God, the Lord is One.

(said quietly) Blessed be the name of the glory of his kingdom forever.

You shall love the Lord your God with all your heart,
with all your soul, and with all your might.
And these words which I command you today
shall be in your heart.
You shall teach them diligently to your children
and you shall speak of them
when you are sitting at home
and when you go on a journey,
when you lie down
and when you rise up.
You shall bind them as a sign on your hand
and they shall be jewels between your eyes.
You shall inscribe them on the doorposts
of your house and on your gates.

LORD'S PRAYER (TRANSLATED FROM GREEK)

Our Father in heaven,
hallowed be your name,
your kingdom come,
your will be done, on earth as in heaven.
Give us today our daily bread.
Forgive us our sins, as we forgive those who sin against us.
Lead us not into temptation,
but deliver us from evil.

SURAH AL-FATIHA (TRANSLATED FROM ARABIC)

In the Name of Allah, the Most Beneficent, the Most Merciful.
All praise to Allah, the Lord of the Universe.
The Most Beneficent, the Most Merciful.
Master of the Day of Judgment.
You (alone) do we worship and of You (only) do we seek help.
Guide us on the Straight Path.
The path of those upon whom You have bestowed Your
bounties, not (the path) of those inflicted with Your anger, nor (of
those) gone astray.

IMAM, RABBI, PRIEST: WHO ARE THEY?

12

In every religion, there are men or women specially chosen to lead and guide believers. These are imams among Muslims, priests and pastors among Christians, and rabbis among Jews. Their roles are very important to their communities.

CALLED

For Muslims, members of the mosque community select an imam. He is chosen for his great knowledge of the Qur'an and has a reputation of being a spiritually wise person. For Jews or Christians, deciding to become a rabbi, priest, or pastor is an internal, spiritual "calling" to this religious position, or vocation. For all, these leaders are recognized as being appointed by God.

Rabbi   Imam

TRAINED

Imams are scholars trained with an in-depth study of the Qur'an as well as Islamic law and other writings, and they show leadership skills in the community. Rabbis usually train for at least five years, studying Jewish texts and traditions in preparation for an examination. On passing, they receive ordination, or semikha, which gives them the authority to be a spiritual guide for a Jewish community. Training for a priest lasts at least five years, studying and preparing for the role. In the Catholic and Orthodox churches, a priest's ordination or admission is a commitment for a life devoted to God and his followers.

MYSTERIOUS...

Some believers decide to live separately from the rest of society in a secluded place to dedicate their whole lives to God and to prayer. They are called monks and nuns. Some live in communities, following a strict way of life.

AND WHY...

are priests just men?

Groups in the Christian churches hold different views about the role of priesthood. For the Catholic and Orthodox churches, only men can become priests because Jesus was a man and priests act on his behalf just like the first apostles, or followers. Catholic priests cannot marry but Orthodox priests can. Both men and women can become priests in some groups within the Protestant Church.

In Arabic, imam means "to stand in the front" because his main role is to lead prayers in a mosque. An imam teaches and people go to him for spiritual guidance and to consult on personal and community matters. A rabbi presides over the services in a synagogue, as well as other roles such as preparing those getting married and training young people. Priests and pastors lead the services, provide spiritual teaching, and care for people in their communities.

✓ TO FIND OUT ABOUT
THE PLACES OF WORSHIP,
GO TO...
18

✓ TO DISCOVER THE KEY STAGES
IN A BELIEVER'S LIFE,
GO TO...
15

How do people become BELIEVERS?

Jews are born Jewish. For Christians, the rite of baptism marks the entry into the church. To become a Muslim, a believer recites the profession of faith, the Shahada. These are rituals to mark a moment, but to be a believer means having a belief.

MOTHER TO SON

The Jewish religion is passed down from mother to son. For children to be considered Jewish, their mothers must be Jewish. Every Jewish child is given a Hebrew name that may be different from their actual name. Eight days after a baby boy is born, a special ceremony is held called Brit Milah. During this the child is circumcised to mark becoming a member of the Jewish people. Baby girls' names are announced in the synagogue on the first Sabbath day after their birth. It is rare to become Jewish as an adult and the training is very long.

Useful words

Circumcision: The removal of the foreskin, often for religious reasons. This is not considered harmful for new-born babies.

WASHED CLEAN

Baptism marks the beginning of a Christian's life as a member of the church. Blessed water is used to symbolize sins being washed away and the beginning of a new life with Jesus Christ. The person becomes a child of God the Father. Sometimes the forehead is marked with holy oil called chrism to show they have been chosen by God. When an infant is baptized, the parents and godparents commit to Christianity on behalf of the child. Some churches baptize people only when they are old enough to decide to believe for themselves. The person is often completely immersed in water, just as Jesus was baptized. This rite of passage is known as a sacrament, an outward sign of when God is spiritually present and based on the words or actions of Jesus.

Useful words:

Shahada: This is the Muslim profession of faith that is often repeated and used during the call to prayer. Translated, it means, "There is no god but God; Muhammad is the messenger of God."

WHISPERED WORDS

At the birth of Muslim children, the words of the Shahada are whispered into their right ear as the first thing they hear. Often their parents also chew a piece of date and rub the juice on the baby's lips as a sweet first taste. After seven days a baby's head is shaved, and the child is given a Muslim name. Baby boys may be circumcised, too. For adults to become a Muslim, they recite the words of the Shahada in front of a witness, committing to believe.

AND WHY...

is a Muslim baby's hair cut?
When the hair is shaved from a Muslim baby, the hair is weighed, and the parents give the weight of their child's hair in gold to the poor. This is one way to give alms, one of the Five Pillars of Islam.

✓ TO FIND OUT THE SIGNS OF THE THREE RELIGIONS, GO TO...
10

✓ TO DISCOVER THE OTHER STAGES OF A BELIEVER'S LIFE, GO TO...
15

14 Is there a school to LEARN ABOUT GOD?

For a believer, belonging to a religion is only the first step. Understanding what to believe and living as a good believer is a continual journey. This can be learned little by little from a young age from parents as well as religious communities.

AT THE SYNAGOGUE

Jewish children from the age of six attend the Talmud Torah at the synagogue. These are classes that teach not only about the texts of the Torah but also about the Jewish traditions and festivals, the Hebrew language, and the history of the Jewish people. The children learn to pray and the boys prepare for their Bar Mitzvah that they will celebrate at the age of thirteen. This ceremony marks their entry into the Jewish community.

Useful words

Catechism: This word, used by Catholic Christians, comes from the Greek meaning "to echo the teaching", for what is learned should be echoed in believers' lives.

AT THE MOSQUE

Muslim children from five years old attend classes at the Madrasa. These are schools organized by mosques where the children learn the Qur'an. In non-Arabic countries they learn to read ancient Arabic, the language in which the Qur'an is written. Then they find out how to recite the Qur'an properly with tajwid, the correct pronunciation. They are also taught how to pray and study the Islamic way of life about fasting and other beliefs and practices.

AT CHURCH

Christian children learn in sessions on Sunday in their local church. They read stories from the Bible to stir their curiosity about God and find out about the life and teachings of Jesus. They also pray and sing songs. As they get older, children study the Bible passages to gain a deeper understanding of their faith and prepare for receiving bread and wine for the first time and confirm their faith. In Catholic churches, children learn the catechism, which are religious questions and answers to gain a better understanding of Catholic beliefs, including the sacraments (see page 45).

CONTINUAL DISCOVERY

Every believer continually discovers new things about their faith as they grow in their relationship with God. Even adults continue to study their holy books, pray, and seek further understanding.

A WORD OF WISDOM

God, who knows best the capacities of men, hide their mysteries to the wise and the prudent of this world and reveals them to the little ones children.

Isaac Newton, famous mathematician and scientist

✓ TO FIND OUT ABOUT PRAYER, GO TO...

11

✓ TO DISCOVER ABOUT THOSE WHO GUIDE BELIEVERS, GO TO...

12

What are
THE IMPORTANT STAGES
in the life of a believer?

Belonging to a religion is both relevant for each day and over a whole lifetime. Religions celebrate special moments in everyone's life with special ceremonies and rites, from birth to death. They remind believers that God is part of their lives.

FROM BIRTH

As soon as a child is born into a religious family, he or she enters the great family of believers. A Jewish baby receives a Hebrew first name eight days after birth, and if a boy, he is circumcised (see page 40). A Muslim baby hears the call to prayer whispered in his or her right ear. A Christian child may be baptized as a baby and so enters the great family of the church.

TO PERSONAL FAITH

Religions celebrate the moment when a child can independently live their lives as a believer. At thirteen years old, a Jewish boy makes his Bar Mitzvah, marking his religious maturity. He is now responsible for following the Jewish commandments. On that day, he receives his tallit (prayer shawl) and a set of tefillin, two small black boxes containing passages from the Torah that go on his forehead and his arm. He reads from the Torah in the synagogue to symbolize his acceptance of the commandments and gives a speech about the Torah. A Jewish girl is twelve when she has her Bat Mitzvah but she may or may not read or give a speech. Muslims do not mark any moment of religious maturity, but from the age of seven, children are invited to practise the five stages of prayer. As they approach puberty around eleven years old, children take part in fasting, which is one of the Five Pillars of Islam. For some Christian children, their stage to mark religious maturity is often when they confirm their faith for themselves at a confirmation service. A bishop lays hands on the child to receive the Holy Spirit.

Useful words:

Sacraments: The sacraments are rites of passage that mark stages of a Christian's life. These moments are based on the words or actions of Jesus. They are an outward sign of when God is spiritually present. The Catholic and Orthodox churches celebrate seven sacraments. Baptism, confirmation, marriage, and a priest's ordination mark the milestones in life. The other three sacraments can be received many times: the Eucharist, which is the receiving of the blessed bread and wine identified as the body and blood of Jesus; reconciliation, when believers ask to be forgiven for their sins; and anointing the sick, to pass on God's strength. Many Protestant churches recognize only the two sacraments: baptism and communion.

MARRIAGE

Many believers want to make the commitment of marriage before God and it is often an important religious occasion. Jews see marriage as a gift from God, marking the beginning of a new home and a new family. The Jewish bride and groom sign a marriage contract called a ketubah, which is also signed by witnesses. The rabbi blesses them under the huppah, a canvas stretched over their heads that represents their future new home. The husband places a ring on the woman's right-hand index finger to mark that they are officially married. In Islam, the groom makes a contract of marriage to his bride, offering a gift, which she receives and consents to in front of witnesses. An imam performs the ceremony, which is called the nikah. Celebrations vary according to local traditions but often passages from the Qur'an are recited and there is a great feast. Christians see marriage as a lifelong partnership blessed by God. In the ceremony, the priest makes sure that the couple are free to marry, then the groom and bride make their vows and exchange rings, and then the priest blesses the union. Orthodox wedding couples are crowned with wreaths as a symbol of glory, representing how they have become king and queen of their new family united by God.

DID YOU KNOW?
Sometimes, at the end of a Jewish wedding ceremony, a groom breaks a wine glass to represent the fragility of marriage.

> **DID YOU KNOW?**
> The Muslim religion and the Jewish religion like to bury their dead in the ground in a simple white cloth. In some countries this is not possible for health reasons and so simple coffins are used.

ETERNAL REST

In every religion, at the end of life there is a final ritual for the dead. For Jews, a candle is lit and placed next to the body from the time of the death to the burial. The body is wrapped in a simple white canvas and the funeral, led by a rabbi, is simple so there is no distinction between rich and poor. Mourners who are close relatives show their grief by making a tear in their clothes level with their heart. For Muslims, the Shahada (profession of faith) is the last words whispered into the ear of the dying person. The dead body is ritually washed and then covered in a shroud, a white cloth sheet called a kafan. The body is laid in the ground on his or her right side, facing towards Mecca. The imam leads the funeral prayers. For Christians, the priest often provides the last rites — a set of prayers — at the dying person's side. The body is placed in a coffin and a funeral service led by the priest is held, often with prayers, readings, and hymns, a reminder of the Christian hope in eternal life. Words about the person's life may be said by a relative. Catholics and other churches pray for the soul of the dead, burn incense to entrust the dead person to God, and light candles in remembrance. Some Orthodox Christians hold a vigil service on the night before the funeral. Funerals vary widely from solemn to noisy expressions of grief.

✓ TO FIND OUT ABOUT RELIGIOUS FESTIVALS, GO TO...
19

✓ TO DISCOVER RELIGIOUS VIEWS ON THE END OF LIFE, GO TO...
23

Does God FORGIVE?

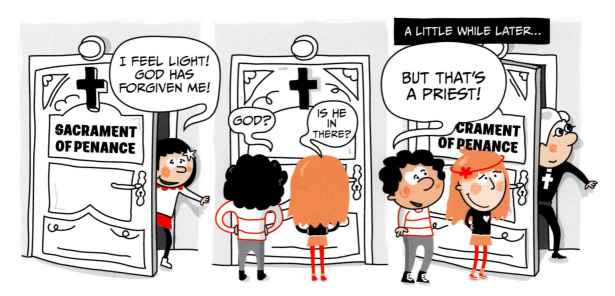

Jews, Christians, and Muslims believe in a God of love who is merciful, meaning that wrongdoings are forgiven. For God to forgive, the person must recognize their wrongdoings and ask for forgiveness.

FORGIVE AND BE FORGIVEN

For Muslims, God is the All Merciful, the Most Forgiving. If the believer regrets their wrongs and changes their behaviour, truly asking God's forgiveness, then they are forgiven. They can implore God through prayer and, by doing good deeds or enduring hardship with patience, receive forgiveness. A Muslim is urged to repent and seek God's forgiveness as soon as possible after doing wrong. Muslims must also forgive or pardon others if they have been wronged by someone. The Qur'an teaches that if an individual does not forgive others, then God will not forgive them. Friday prayer is an important moment for forgiveness, for if believers do their ablutions, pray at the mosque, and listen to the imam's sermon in silence, then God forgives the wrongs committed between Fridays.

A BLESSED DAY

Throughout the history of the Jewish people, God never stops forgiving his people and showing them love. Jews believe in a God who wants to forgive them. They need to repent sincerely for their wrongdoings through prayer and promise not to do wrong in the same way again. If they have done wrong to another person, they must ask for forgiveness and pay for the hurt caused. In addition, they can earn forgiveness by doing good deeds. Each year a solemn and important day is held called Yom Kippur, the Day of Atonement (Great Forgiveness). Jews fast and reflect on their actions over the past year, confessing their wrongs to God. They take new resolutions, promising not to wrong in the same way again and begging God's forgiveness. That day is also an opportunity to reconcile and apologize to others.

SAVED

Christians believe Jesus died on the cross for their sins, so that new life can be received and restored with God. This is called salvation. Now, God freely forgives all people. To receive God's forgiveness, Jesus taught people to confess (admit) what they have done wrong and truly repent (say sorry). He also said that as believers have received God's complete forgiveness so they must forgive others completely if wrong is done to them. Many Christians pray directly to God, asking for forgiveness through Jesus. In the Catholic Church, believers confess their wrongs to a priest, who forgives them in the name of Jesus. This is called the sacrament of penance.

Useful words:

Ablutions: Before prayer, Muslims wash themselves in a certain way to prepare their minds and clean their bodies. They wash their hands, mouth, nose, face, arms to the elbow, head, ears, neck, and feet.

Mercy: Mercy comes from a combination of two Latin words that mean "to have pity, kindness" and "heart". God's mercy to forgive is because of great love.

✓ TO FIND OUT ABOUT VIEWS ON EVIL, GO TO...
24

✓ TO DISCOVER WHAT FASTING IS FOR, GO TO...
21

17 WHICH DAY IS SPECIAL?

In each religion, there is one day especially dedicated to God. This day is set apart for spending more time in God's presence. This sacred day is different for each religion. The day often involves bringing people together. Meeting weekly helps them to build relationships as a community.

FRIDAY

Among Muslims, Friday is the most important day of the week. For them, this was the day when God created the first man, Adam. They also believe that this is the day on which the Day of Judgment will take place at the end of times. So, Friday is the chosen day to gather as a community. All men are expected to come together at the mosque for midday prayers. Women can pray at home or at the mosque. The imam gives a sermon (talk) and then leads the prayers. To prepare for going to the mosque, believers take a bath and the men shave or trim their beards and wear clean, usually white, clothes. They do not hurry but take care to arrive on time. After attending the mosque, they can eat, and often this is a special meal to celebrate.

MYSTERIOUS...

For most Muslims, Fridays are not a day off. The midday prayers only last about three-quarters of an hour, so that worshippers can return to work. For Muslims who have jobs where others' lives depend on them, such as doctors, they are not obliged to attend Friday prayers.

SATURDAY

Judaism is the only religion that has a weekly festival, Shabbat, remembering the seventh day of creation when God rested. This is a day of rest for many Jews and begins every Friday at sunset and ends the following Saturday night when three stars appear in the sky. To begin the Shabbat, the woman of the house lights the special candles and says a blessing. Shabbat is a day dedicated to prayer and reading the Torah and is joyfully celebrated as a family and community. Guests may be invited to the Friday evening meal. Worshippers go to the synagogue on Friday evening and on Saturday morning and afterwards share a meal that has often been kept warm overnight. No work is allowed on Shabbat, including cooking, lighting a fire, or even writing. The end of Shabbat is marked by lighting a candle with several twisted wicks, blessing a cup of wine, and smelling sweet spices in a ceremony called havdalah. This symbolizes the separation of the holy Shabbat and the other days of the week.

AND WHY...

are candles lit for Shabbat?
Thousands of years ago, Sarah the wife of Abraham lit candles in their tent on Friday night. Candles create a lovely atmosphere in a home and provide a sense of peace, which are important for Shabbat. The lit candles also remind believers of the existence of God, who shines in their lives.

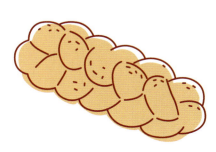

SUNDAY

Christians think of Sunday as the Lord's Day. This was the day that Jesus, who is at the centre of their faith, was resurrected (raised to life) three days after his death on a cross. Christians often gather to worship. They listen to several texts from the Bible and then a priest or pastor talks about the passages in a sermon. They sing and pray. For many Christians, the central part of the service is to commemorate Jesus' last meal with his apostles, when Jesus instructed them to remember him through the taking of bread and wine as his body and blood. Christians are invited to participate in this meal, which the Catholic Church calls Mass or Eucharist, the Orthodox Church calls Holy Liturgy, and the Protestant Church may call Holy Communion or the Lord's Supper.

Useful words

Host: The holy bread of Mass or Holy Communion is called a "host". This is usually a thin round wafer. After the priest blesses and repeats the words and actions of Jesus, Catholics believe that Christ's body is actually present in the bread.

✓ TO FIND OUT ABOUT PRAYER, GO TO...

11

✓ TO DISCOVER PLACES OF WORSHIP, GO TO...

18

18 What does A PLACE OF WORSHIP look like?

Each religion has a special place dedicated to God, called either a synagogue, a church, or a mosque, and each is a sacred place of worship. Although some are beautiful and inspiring buildings, they are built to encourage prayer and to make believers feel closer to God. There is no set design for a synagogue, mosque, or church, so how they look can be very varied.

TOWARDS JERUSALEM

The Jewish synagogue is built around a raised platform called the bimah from where the Torah is read. Positioned on a wall that faces Jerusalem is the holiest place in the synagogue, the Ark. This is a cupboard where the Torah scrolls are stored. The Ark is hidden by a curtain and in front hangs a lamp that is always lit, reminding believers of God's eternal presence.

FACING MECCA

Muslim communities gather in mosques. A mosque consists of a large prayer hall, a courtyard to read or meditate in, and traditionally a thin tower called a minaret. The prayer hall contains no statue or image, but there is a raised platform called a minbar from which the imam speaks. There is also a semi-circular niche in a wall called a mihrab that shows the direction of Mecca, and Muslims face this when praying as the imam leads the prayers. The call to prayer is made by the muezzin, who traditionally stood at the highest point of a mosque in the minaret before the use of loudspeakers. Believers enter the mosque barefoot to be respectful before God. They make their ablutions (wash) at the fountain in the courtyard and then enter the prayer hall.

DID YOU KNOW?
Before entering a mosque, shoes are removed so dirt from the streets is not brought into this holy place and to be clean before God. To go into a synagogue, it is Jewish tradition to cover the head as a sign of humility before God. In a church, it is considered respectful for a man to remove his hat.

FOCUS ON CHRIST

The word "church" means a community of Christian believers, but it is also used as the name for the building where many Christians worship. Churches vary in shape and size and some can be very elaborate. From the air, some churches are in the shape of a cross with a long nave where the congregation sit, a chancel or sanctuary where a table called the altar is positioned, and side chapels for private prayer. The altar is where the priest or pastor stands to bless the bread and wine. There is often a lectern – a tall book stand from where the Bible is read. The preacher may also stand to deliver their sermon (talk) from a raised position called the pulpit. In many churches, behind the altar is a screen, painting, or carved altarpiece decorated with scenes from the Bible or images of saintly figures or heaven.

AND WHY...
are some churches called cathedrals?
Cathedral is a Latin word for "seat". Some Christian groups have bishops as a higher position than priests, who oversee a diocese, or large group of churches in an area. The main church of the diocese or "seat" of a bishop is called a cathedral.

✓ TO FIND OUT ABOUT THOSE WHO LEAD WORSHIP, GO TO...
12

✓ TO DISCOVER WHEN THESE PLACES ARE USED, GO TO...
17

GUIDED TOUR

◆ ◆ ◆

An example of a church plan

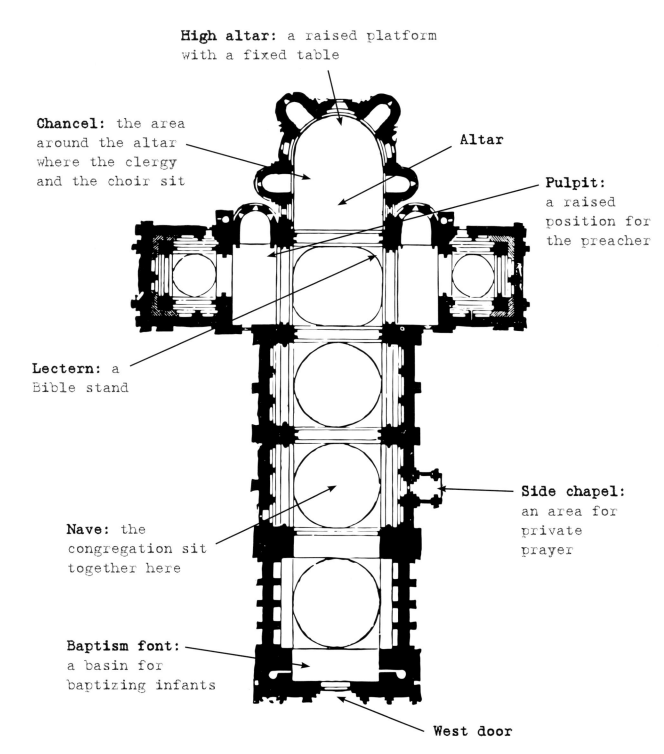

Inside a synagogue

Men and women are separated in the synagogue. Often women sit in the balcony.

Menorah: seven-branched candlestick as a reminder of the Temple of Jerusalem

Eternal Light

Torah scrolls

Holy Ark on the wall facing Jerusalem

Bimah: a raised stage with a reading table

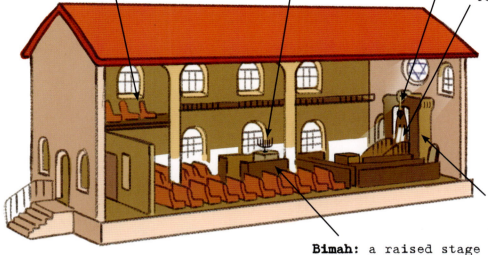

Layout of a mosque

Mihrab: a niche indicating the direction of Mecca

Five times a day, the muezzin goes up the minaret to give the call to prayer. Today loudspeakers are often used instead.

Minbar: a platform on which the imam stands to speak and lead prayers

Minaret

Prayer hall

Fountain or pool for ablutions

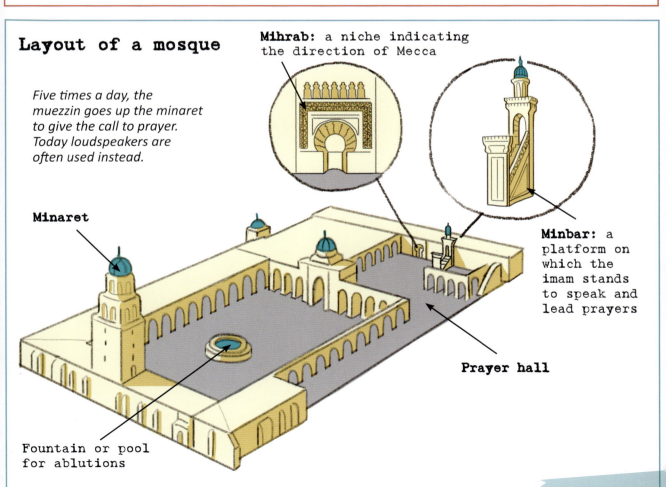

When do they celebrate FESTIVALS?

Throughout the year, there are religious festivals that bring together believers as a family or a community. Every festival is linked to an event in history or to various rituals for connecting with God. Many religious festivals change their dates each year based on the position of the sun or moon.

ASH WEDNESDAY

The forty-day period of Lent begins on a Wednesday and leads up to the main Christian festival of Easter. At the start of Lent, some Christians attend a service to receive a mark of ash on the forehead to show their humility before God. Lent is a reflective time for devotion to God through prayer and study. Originally Christians used to fast (not eat), remembering the time that Jesus withdrew to the desert for forty days. Nowadays they may give up something to test their commitment to God.

HOLY WEEK

Each year, Christians relive the last week of Jesus' life. This begins on Palm Sunday, remembering the arrival of Jesus into Jerusalem riding on a donkey. Holy Thursday recalls Jesus' last meal and his arrest. Good Friday is the day of Jesus' death on a cross. Easter is the day of celebration of Jesus' resurrection. For some churches, this begins on Saturday night and for others at sunrise on Sunday.

DID YOU KNOW?

The egg is a symbol of renewal and life. It has become tradition to buy eggs to celebrate the resurrection of Jesus.

PURIM

Purim is a Jewish festival that remembers a moment in the history of the Jewish people. It celebrates the courage of Queen Esther, who prevented the massacre of the Jewish people by the Persians. Jews read the story and then have a fun festival, recalling the celebrations of the Jews after being saved.

PASSOVER

The Jewish festival of Passover remembers the start of the Jewish nation, when the Hebrew people left Egypt led by Moses and crossed the Red Sea on dry ground. Jews celebrate with a meal called a seder. The meal includes roasted lamb, which the Hebrews ate on the night before they left; bitter herbs, to symbolize the tears of suffering as slaves in Egypt; and matzos, which is flat bread with no yeast, to remember how the Hebrews left in a hurry, taking bread that had not risen. The story is read, and they sing praises to God.

LAILAT AL MIRAJ

The Muslim festival Lailat al Miraj celebrates Muhammad's night journey from Mecca to Jerusalem where he ascended to heaven. He rode on a strange winged creature called Buraq in the company of archangel Gabriel. Many Muslims spend the night at the mosque in prayer. This journey of the soul is read from the Qur'an and Muslims remember Muhammad being filled with purity and wisdom before meeting God.

PENTECOST

Ten days after Jesus ascended into heaven promising his apostles that he would send a helper, they received the Holy Spirit. They went out onto the streets to tell people about Jesus. This festival is Pentecost, marking the birthday of the Christian church.

SHAVUOT

Fifty days after Passover, Jews celebrate another harvest festival called Shavuot or Feast of Weeks. This marks the time that God gave the Torah to Moses on Mount Sinai. Overnight they read the Torah, and everyone tries to stay awake.

DID YOU KNOW?
The breakfast on Eid al-Fitr includes eating dates because Muhammad ate seven a day for nourishment. He called the date the "fruit of Paradise".

EID AL-FITR

The Muslim feast of Eid al-Fitr marks the end of Ramadan. Ramadan is a month-long period of fasting between sunrise and sunset. For the festival, Muslims take a ritual bath, put on their best or new clothes, eat a good breakfast, decorate their homes, and pray at the mosque. They thank God for strength through the time of fasting, give alms to the poor, and try to meet as many people as possible to share good wishes.

Useful words:
Eid: This is an Arabic word meaning "party".

Shofar: This long instrument is made from a ram's horn. A hundred notes are blown at the Jewish feast of Rosh Hashanah.

EID AL-ADHA

Also known as Eid al-Kabir, Eid al-Adha is "the Feast of Sacrifice" and remembers the day when Ibrahim was about to sacrifice his son. God stopped him and gave a ram instead. Muslims sacrifice a sheep or goat and share out the meat equally between family, friends, and the poor. This festival also marks the end of the hajj, the pilgrimage to Mecca.

ROSH HASHANAH

This festival marks the beginning of the Jewish New Year, remembering God's creation of the world, and Adam and Eve. The story of the sacrifice of Isaac is also remembered. It marks the beginning of a ten-day time of judgment when Jews believe God opens a book and decides what the next year will be like for them.

AL-HIJRA

This day is the beginning of the Islamic New Year, remembering Muhammad's move from Mecca to Medina to set up the first Islamic state.

YOM KIPPUR

Ten days after Rosh Hashanah, Yom Kippur is "the Day of Atonement" and is one of the most important days in the Jewish calendar. Jews fast, with no food or drink for twenty-five hours, dress simply, and do not wash. At the synagogue, believers confess their wrongs and ask God's forgiveness. The day ends with a service to mark God sealing the book of judgment for the next year.

SUKKOT

The week-long Jewish festival Sukkot remembers the forty years that the Hebrew people spent wandering in the desert after they left Egypt on their way to God's promised land. A sukkah is traditionally a hut. Every family builds a sukkah in their garden or on a balcony in which to stay. In the synagogue they bless four plants – a palm, an etrog (citrus fruit), a myrtle, and a willow – waving them in all directions to show that God is everywhere.

ALL SAINTS' DAY

This is a Christian festival that remembers those who have lived as saints, doing good works and dying as martyrs for their faith. The next day is All Souls' Day, when Christians commemorate those who have died.

MAWLID

This Muslim festival remembers the birth of Prophet Muhammad. This is an opportunity to tell children about his life.

CHRISTMAS AND THE EPIPHANY

Christmas is a Christian festival celebrating the birth of Jesus, including the joy of the shepherds' visit. Twelve days later, the day of Epiphany remembers the visit of the Magi who came from the East to worship Jesus.

HANUKKAH

This is the Jewish festival of lights, celebrating an important historical event when the Temple in Jerusalem was rededicated after a successful rebellion by the Maccabees. The Jewish people could practise their faith again. The menorah, or seven-branched candlestick, in the Temple only had enough oil to burn for one day, but miraculously it lasted for eight days. A candle is lit on each night of the festival.

AND WHY...

is Jesus' birth celebrated on 25 December?
The date of Jesus' exact birth is unknown. Christians chose this date as the days begin to lengthen after the winter solstice (the shortest day of the year). This symbolizes the return to light.

DID YOU KNOW?

Used by most of the world, the Gregorian calendar uses Jesus' birth more than 2,000 years ago as its starting point. Jews date their calendar to the creation of Adam, more than 5,700 years ago. The Muslim calendar begins in the year that Muhammad took his followers from Mecca to Medina and so is 622 years behind the Gregorian year date.

✓ TO FIND OUT THE STORY OF THE RELIGIONS, GO TO...

6

✓ TO DISCOVER THE MOST IMPORTANT DAY OF THE WEEK, GO TO...

17

20 Does everyone give PRESENTS AT CHRISTMAS?

Walking through the streets in December, it is difficult not to be aware that Christmas is coming. There are gifts to buy, fir trees to decorate, and Santa Claus is everywhere. All the world seems to be about to celebrate Christmas.

THE BIRTH OF JESUS

Christmas is a religious holiday for Christians. They celebrate the birth of Jesus in the town of Bethlehem more than 2,000 years ago. Christians prepare for Christmas through a four-week period called Advent. They often go to church on Christmas Eve or Christmas Day, enjoy a festive meal, and give presents to each other. However, Christmas is celebrated even by people who do not practise this religion. Some people have lost its meaning and only retain the idea of giving and receiving gifts and spending time with family.

Useful words:

Advent: the beginning of the Christian church year. The four Sundays before Christmas are a time of preparation for the coming of Jesus.

NOT FOR ALL

Most Jews do not celebrate Christmas or give each other gifts. In Judaism, the festival of Hanukkah often falls in the month of December. At this festival of light, children receive gifts. For Muslims, Jesus is a prophet, so some celebrate his birth on 25 December. This is not a religious festival, though, and there is unlikely to be an exchange of presents. The festival Eid al-Fitr at the end of the fasting month of Ramadan is the time when Muslims give presents to children.

MYSTERIOUS...

The wise men that visited Jesus brought with them three gifts that seem a strange choice to give to a child. The first was gold to symbolize kingship. The second was frankincense to symbolize a priestly role. The third gift was myrrh used to prepare a dead body. Christians believe each gift reflected the roles of Jesus as King, Priest of God, and Saviour.

✓ TO DISCOVER WHO JESUS IS, GO TO...

5

✓ TO FIND OUT ABOUT OTHER RELIGIOUS FESTIVALS, GO TO...

19

21 ARE LENT AND RAMADAN
the same thing?

Lent and Ramadan seem similar. They are both times when believers fast, which means to have no food. This is a time to focus on God by putting him before anything else. But the practice of Lent and Ramadan is very different.

PREPARATION FOR EASTER

The period of Lent lasts for forty days leading up to Easter, the day when Christians celebrate the resurrection (raising to life) of Jesus. During these forty days, believers prepare for Easter through prayer, sharing and giving, and traditionally fasting. Christians often dedicate more time to prayer and Bible study. They may fast and go without food on the first day of Lent and on Fridays, especially Good Friday, when they remember Jesus' death. Sharing means that they are more attentive to those who have nothing, just as Jesus taught. These are the principles of Lent but there are no specific rules, so believers are free to follow their consciences as they journey towards Easter.

GOD BEFORE THE BODY

Ramadan is a month-long fast for Muslims, which means they do not eat or drink between sunrise and sunset. This is one of the Five Pillars of Islam so is an obligation for all believers after puberty. The rules are a lot stricter than those of Lent and the whole Muslim community takes part. In the hours of darkness, Muslims can eat and drink a simple meal. The fast aims to help believers focus on God, but believers are also expected to read the Qur'an and pray more. Ramadan ends with a three-day festival, Eid ul-Fitr, when Muslims celebrate, bless each other, and give alms (money or food) to the poor.

MYSTERIOUS

Jewish people also have seven separate days of fasting. One of these days is Yom Kippur, the Day of Atonement. Believers fast and ask forgiveness of God for all their wrongdoings. For each of the three religions, fasting is a way to refocus on God, show humility, and depend upon God.

AND WHY...

do small children not fast?

Not eating or drinking is not dangerous if the time of fasting is not long, as in the case of Lent and Ramadan. However, children's bodies are not adapted to being deprived of food for long, so they do not fast. Also, people who are sick and pregnant women are not expected to fast. Religions do not put the most vulnerable at risk.

✓ TO FIND OUT WHY BELIEVERS FAST,
GO TO..
16

✓ TO DISCOVER WHAT CAN OR CANNOT BE EATEN,
GO TO..
22

22 CAN BELIEVERS EAT
what they like?

When it comes to food, Christians are free to eat whatever they want. However, for Jews and Muslims there are rules for what they can and cannot eat.

HALAL FOOD

In Islam there are two restrictions for Muslims: they are not allowed to eat pork or drink alcohol. Pork is declared unclean by God, but other meat can be eaten if it has been killed in a certain way according to the Qur'an. This meat is called halal. Alcohol is forbidden as it confuses the mind.

Useful words

Kosher: This term in Hebrew means "fit" or "proper".
Halal: This Arabic word means "lawful".

KOSHER FOOD

There are many more banned foods in Jewish laws as set in the Torah and so commanded by God. The food that can be eaten is called kosher. Animals that have cloven hooves and chew the cud, such as lambs and cattle can be eaten, but pork cannot be eaten. Fish with fins and scales can be eaten but crustaceans such as shrimp and crabs cannot. All fruit and vegetables must be checked carefully that no insects are on them as they are non-kosher. The laws allowed kosher wine made from grapes from a vineyard that follows the rules in the Torah can be drunk. These rules help Jews remember that God created the world and humans do not have the right to do everything they want. Even today, Orthodox Jews follow the kosher laws but some Jews interpret them differently.

AND WHY...

do some Christians eat fish on Fridays?
In the past, the church forbade the eating of meat on Fridays because this was considered a rich person's food. The simpler dish of fish was eaten instead. This tradition is disappearing, especially as fish has become more expensive.

✓ TO FIND OUT WHERE THE FOOD BANS ARE WRITTEN, GO TO...

6

✓ TO DISCOVER THE OTHER COMMANDS OF GOD, GO TO...

8

23 What happens AFTER DEATH?

Jews, Christians, and Muslims believe that death is not the end of everything and there is a promise of being resurrected, meaning "to be alive again" forever. This gives believers great hope!

END OF EARTHLY LIFE

For believers of all three religions, death means the end of their lives on earth. They do not believe in reincarnation, which means coming back as another person or animal. Instead, they believe in resurrection, which is completely different.

AND THE BEGINNING OF A NEW LIFE

After death, Jews, Christians, and Muslims believe that God promises another life where believers will be with God and know infinite happiness. They believe that they will be resurrected with a new body. Christians especially believe this, as Jesus was raised from the dead and appeared to his friends and even ate with them.

BUT

Christians believe that when Jesus died on the cross, he defeated death and paid the price for all the sins of the world, and then he was raised to life. As followers of Christ, they believe that only through Jesus and living their lives his way, will they be given eternal life. For Muslims, if they have done more good deeds than bad in their lives and fulfilled their Islamic obligations, then they will be resurrected. For Jews, if believers have led good lives according to God's commandments, then they deserve eternal life.

A WORD OF WISDOM

"Death can be something beautiful. It is like going home. He who dies in God... has gone home to God."

Saint Theresa of Calcutta

✓ TO FIND OUT HOW THE DEAD ARE BURIED, GO TO...

15

✓ TO DISCOVER HOW RELIGIONS UNDERSTAND GOD, GO TO...

3

Hell or heaven?

◆◆◆

At the end of times, believers from all three religions think that there will be a great Day of Judgment. God will judge them on how they lived their earthly lives.

Heaven

For Muslims, those who perform more good deeds than bad will enter Jannah, or Paradise. This is described as a "garden of everlasting bliss" where there will be no sickness, pain, or sadness. For Jews, the afterlife is called Olam Ha-ba, meaning "world to come", which is a heavenly Garden of Eden. For Christians, the last book of the Bible, called Revelation, describes a glorious new city of Jerusalem coming down from heaven where believers will be reunited with Jesus Christ.

Hell

Christians believe that God created humans to have free will and a choice to follow him. If they do not follow God, which is considered evil, then they will be judged and go to hell. No one knows what hell is like, but believers think there will be suffering, as people would be separated from God and his love. Muslims call this place Jahannam. Most Jews do not believe in the existence of hell.

Purgatory

Jews believe that after their death there will be a period of twelve months in a process called purgatory to purify themselves before they can be with God. Catholic Christians also believe in a place called purgatory, where a believer who has not rejected God but is not yet ready prepares for entering eternal life with God.

· 71 ·

24 Does THE DEVIL exist?

Jews and Christians use the name Satan. Muslims call him Iblis. He is also the Seducer, the Tempter, Lucifer, the Adversary… Whatever the Devil's name, many believers think that he exists and tempts humans to do wrong.

DISOBEDIENCE

According to the Qur'an, God drove out Iblis from Paradise after he refused to bow to Adam, the first man. Iblis claimed he was nobler because he was created by God out of fire, but Adam came only from clay. Iblis' pride meant he disobeyed God. In revenge for being thrown out, Iblis tests humans by tempting them away from obedience to God. The Prophet Muhammad warned Muslims about Iblis, also known as Shaitan, who tries to divert them from worshipping God. For Jews and Christians, Satan is known as a "fallen angel" who rebelled against God before the creation of humans. In all three religions, there is the story that the first woman, Eve, was tempted to eat forbidden fruit in the Garden of Eden, causing both Adam and Eve to be banished.

✓ TO FIND OUT ABOUT HOW TO BE A GOOD BELIEVER, GO TO…

8

✓ TO DISCOVER IF HELL EXISTS, GO TO…

23

And do they all believe in angels?

◆◆◆

The Torah, the Bible, and the Qur'an all mention appearances of angels. Angels are messengers of God. They are spiritual beings that are only seen when they appear to people to deliver a message from God.

GENESIS, CHAPTER 28 IN THE TORAH

"[Jacob] dreamed and behold! A ladder set up on the ground and its top reached to heaven; and behold, angels of God were ascending and descending upon it."

SURAH FATIR 35 of QUR'AN

"[All] praise is [due] to Allah, Creator of the heavens and the earth, [who] made the angels messengers having wings, two or three or four. He increases in creation what He wills. Indeed, Allah is over all things competent."

God sent the angel Gabriel to Nazareth, a town in Galilee, to a virgin pledged to be married to a man named Joseph, a descendant of David. The virgin's name was Mary. The angel went to her and said, "Greetings, you who are highly favored! The Lord is with you."

Mary was greatly troubled at his words and wondered what kind of greeting this might be. But the angel said to her, "Do not be afraid, Mary; you have found favor with God. You will conceive and give birth to a son, and you are to call him Jesus."

GOSPEL OF LUKE IN THE BIBLE, CHAPTER 1

25 Which is THE RIGHT RELIGION?

If you ask a Jew, a Christian, or a Muslim which is the right religion, most will say that it is theirs. Religion is a way of life and believers consider their religion the right way to relate to their God.

HEART OF A BELIEVER

Being a believer is not about following rituals and a set of rules without thinking. What matters is their heart before their God; finding delight, purpose, and truth, as they follow their practices, learn about their beliefs, celebrate, and worship. This faithful heart then radiates out to those around them in the way they live and help others.

DIALOGUE

Today, representatives of the three religions meet regularly to talk, to seek to understand each other, accept their differences, and learn to get along. This is known as "multi-faith or interfaith dialogue". They look at what they can do to work together on the things they share in common, such as promoting peace, seeking justice, and helping those who suffer. They respect and collaborate with each other, leading to friendship, even though they believe different things.

DID YOU KNOW?

In 1970, religious leaders and representatives from around the world came together to form Religions for Peace to promote peace among religious communities. The movement's principles include respecting religious differences; acting on deeply held and widely shared values; preserving the identity of each religious community, and respecting the different ways religious communities are organized.

MORE USEFUL WORDS

Alms: money or food given to the poor.

Ascended: a soul or spiritual being raised to heaven.

Atonement: repayment for sin to enable reconciliation with God. Christians believe this was made possible through Jesus Christ.

Baptism: a Christian rite of sprinkling or being immersed in water symbolizing entering the church.

Believer: a person who follows a particular religion and has religious faith.

Commandments: a set of instructions or laws by God about how to live.

Confession: an acknowledgment of sins and seeking absolution (forgiveness).

Day of Judgment: an act of examining thoughts and deeds by God at the end of times.

Evangelical: this word comes from the Greek meaning "the good news", and the focus is on the gospel of Jesus, including sharing the faith, practised by the Protestant Church.

Faith: a spiritual confidence and trust in a set of religious beliefs, rather than proof.

Fasting: going without food and drink.

Five Pillars of Islam: the five duties expected of every Muslim: profession of faith, ritual prayer, giving alms, fasting during Ramadan, and pilgrimage to Mecca.

Forgiveness or absolution: a complete release from guilt or punishment.

Obligation: something a person is morally or legally required to do. For believers, this is as a duty or commitment to their religion.

Religion: the belief in an unseen higher power and the set of practices followed for worship.

Resurrection: the raising from death to life.

Revelation: the revealing of future events by God to humans.

Ritual: a religious practice with a series of actions in a certain order.

Sacrifice: an offering to an unseen higher power that could sometimes involve killing an animal or a person.

Salvation: the act of being delivered from sin and its consequences believed by Christians to be made possible by faith in Jesus Christ.

Sin: an action of wrongdoing that is against God's law.

Worship: an act of showing adoration and praise to God.

Index

The references given relate to the chapter numbers.

A
Abraham 1, 2, 4, 7, 17
Al-Hijra 19
Allah 2, 3, 11, 24
Angel 1, 4, 6, 7, 19, 24

B
Baptism 13, 15
Bar Mitzvah 14, 15
Bible 6, 14, 17
Brit Milah 13

C
Catechism 6, 14
Children 13, 14, 15, 19, 20, 21
Christmas 19, 20
Church 15, 17, 18
Circumcision 13, 15
Commandments 5, 6, 7, 8, 15, 23
Crescent 10
Cross 10

D
Death 15, 23
Devil 24

E
Easter 19, 21
Eid al-Fitr 19, 20, 21
Eid al-Adha 19
Eucharist 15

F
Festivals 19
Five Pillars of Islam 8, 9, 10, 11, 13, 15, 21
Forgiveness 16, 19
Friday 16, 17, 19, 21, 22

G
Funeral 15

Gentile 5
Gospel 2, 6, 24

H
Halal 22
Hanukkah 19
HaShem 3
Heaven 1, 7, 10, 11, 19, 23, 24
Hell 23
Holy Spirit 2, 3, 10, 15, 19

I
Imam 2, 12, 15, 18
Isaac and Ishmael 1, 4, 7, 19
Israel 1, 7

J
Jacob 1, 7
Jerusalem 7, 18, 19, 23
Jesus 1, 2, 3, 5, 6, 7, 8, 10, 11,
                              12, 17, 19, 20, 21, 23

K
Kosher 22

L
Lailat al Miraj 19
Lent 19, 21
Lord's Prayer 11

M
Madrasa 14
Marriage 15
Mary 1, 5, 7, 24
Mass 17
Mawlid 19

Mecca 7, 8, 9, 11, 18, 19
Menorah 10, 18, 19
Messiah 1, 5
Minaret 18
Mitzvot 8
Monotheism 1, 2
Moses 3, 6, 7, 8, 19
Mosque 7, 9, 12, 14, 16, 17, 18, 19
Muezzin 18
Muhammad 1, 2, 6, 7, 8, 10, 19, 24

N
New Testament 6

O
Old Testament 6

P
Passover 5, 9, 19
Pastor 12, 17, 18
Pilgrimage 7, 8, 9
Pope 7
Prayer 11
Priest 12, 15, 16, 17, 18
Prophet 1, 5
Purim 19

Q
Qur'an 6, 11, 14, 21, 24

R
Rabbi 12
Ramadan 15, 19, 20, 21
Resurrection 5, 17, 19, 20, 21, 23
Rome 7
Rosh Hashanah 19

S
Sacrament 13, 14, 15, 16
Saturday 17
Shabbat 8, 17
Shahada 13, 15
Shavuot 19
Shema 2, 11
Sign of the cross 10
Son of God 1, 3, 5, 10
Star (of David) 10
Sukkot 9, 19
Sunday 17
Surah 2, 6, 11
Synagogue 14, 15, 17, 18

T
Talmud 6, 8, 14
Tefillin 11, 15
Temple of Jerusalem ... 5, 7, 9, 10, 18, 19
Ten Commandments 7, 8
Torah 3, 5, 6, 8, 11, 14, 15, 17, 18
Trinity 2, 3

V, W, Y
Vatican 7
Wailing Wall 7
Yom Kippur 16, 19, 21

Other illustrations: Eve Grosset

Illustrations Shutterstock.com :

Page 14 : © museyushaya
Page 15 : © Lukasz Stefanski
Page 17 : © pimlena
Page 21 : © museyushaya, © galaira
Page 22: © Umm Leena
Page 31 : © SAHAS2015
Pages 32-33 : © museyushaya, © konstantinks, © Vdant85 © Mr. Rashad
Page 37 : © Gil C
Page 38 : © Yustus
Page 46 : © onot
Page 52 : © infini
Page 56 : © Morphart Creation
Page 68 : © musmellow
Page 71 : © VikiVector

INVESTIGATE: UNDERSTANDING GOD

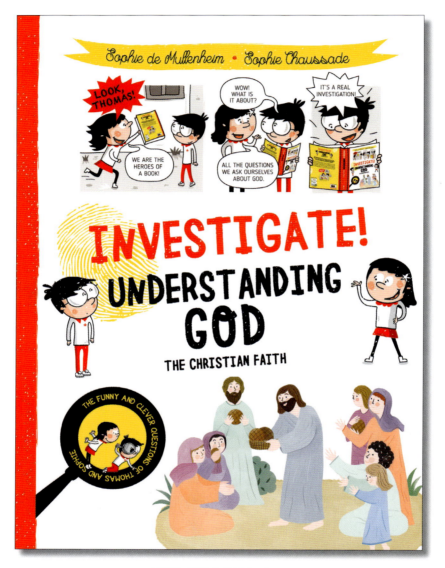

ISBN: 978 0 74597 945 8